50 French Cake Recipes

By: Kelly Johnson

Table of Contents

- Tarte Tatin
- Madeleines
- Mille-Feuille
- Paris-Brest
- Financier
- Clafoutis
- Opera Cake
- Gâteau Basque
- Gâteau Saint-Honoré
- Chiffon Cake
- Tarte au Citron
- Gâteau de Mamie
- Gâteau au Yaourt
- Baba au Rhum
- Tartelette au Chocolat
- Kouign-Amann
- Dacquoise

- Mousse au Chocolat Cake
- Gâteau de Savoie
- Gâteau au Miel
- Cannelé
- Galette des Rois
- Gâteau Bourdaloue
- Tarte aux Poires
- Cake de Pâques
- Pithiviers
- Tarte au Praliné
- Pain d'Épices
- Tarte aux Fruits Rouges
- Moelleux au Chocolat
- Crêpe Cake
- Flan Parisien
- Soufflé au Chocolat
- Tarte aux Noix de Pécan
- Gâteau Opéra
- Quatre-Quarts

- Charlotte aux Fraises
- Mousse au Pistache Cake
- Tarte Normande
- Biscuit Joconde
- Tarte Bourdaloue
- Pâte de Fruit Cake
- Chouquette Cake
- Gâteau à la Crème de Marrons
- Tarte aux Citron Vert
- Flaugnarde
- Gâteau au Chocolat et à la Crème Fraîche
- Savarin
- Tarte au Caramel Beurre Salé
- Tarte à la Crème Pâtissière

Tarte Tatin

Ingredients:

- 6 large apples (preferably Granny Smith or Golden Delicious)
- 100 g butter
- 200 g sugar
- 1 sheet puff pastry
- 1 tsp vanilla extract

Instructions:
Preheat oven to 190°C (375°F).
Peel and core the apples, cutting them into halves or quarters.
In an oven-safe skillet, melt butter and sugar over medium heat, stirring constantly until the mixture turns into a golden caramel.
Arrange the apple slices on top of the caramel in a circular pattern.
Cook for 10 minutes on the stovetop to soften the apples.
Roll out the puff pastry and place it over the apples, tucking the edges in around the pan.
Bake for 30–35 minutes, or until the pastry is golden.
Remove from the oven, let cool slightly, and carefully flip the tart onto a plate.
Serve warm with vanilla ice cream or whipped cream.

Madeleines

Ingredients:

- 120 g flour
- 100 g sugar
- 2 large eggs
- 100 g butter, melted
- 1 tsp vanilla extract
- 1 tsp lemon zest
- 1 tsp baking powder
- A pinch of salt

Instructions:

Preheat oven to 180°C (350°F) and grease a madeleine pan.
Whisk eggs and sugar together until pale and fluffy.
Fold in the flour, baking powder, salt, and lemon zest.
Stir in the melted butter and vanilla extract.
Spoon the batter into the madeleine molds, filling each about halfway.
Bake for 10–12 minutes until golden and the edges are slightly crisp.
Let them cool slightly before serving.

Mille-Feuille

Ingredients:

- 2 sheets puff pastry
- 500 ml heavy cream
- 2 tbsp sugar
- 1 tsp vanilla extract
- 1 tbsp cornstarch
- 1 egg yolk
- 100 g icing sugar

Instructions:

Preheat oven to 200°C (400°F).
Roll out puff pastry and bake according to package instructions, then allow it to cool.
Whisk together the cream, sugar, vanilla, cornstarch, and egg yolk in a saucepan.
Cook over medium heat until thickened, stirring constantly.
Allow the cream to cool, then pipe it onto one sheet of puff pastry.
Place the second sheet of puff pastry on top.
Dust with icing sugar and cut into rectangles.
Serve chilled.

Paris-Brest

Ingredients:

- **Choux Pastry:** 250 ml water, 100 g butter, 150 g flour, 3 eggs, 1 pinch of salt

- **Cream Filling:** 500 ml milk, 100 g sugar, 4 egg yolks, 40 g cornstarch, 1 tsp vanilla extract, 200 ml whipped cream

Instructions:

Preheat oven to 180°C (350°F).
For the choux pastry, bring water, butter, and salt to a boil.
Remove from heat and stir in the flour.
Return to low heat and stir until the dough forms a ball.
Let cool slightly, then beat in the eggs one at a time.
Spoon the dough into a piping bag and pipe a large ring onto a baking sheet.
Bake for 25–30 minutes until golden.
For the cream filling, whisk together sugar, egg yolks, cornstarch, and milk in a saucepan.
Cook over medium heat until thickened, then cool.
Whip the cream and fold into the cooled custard.
Cut the choux pastry ring in half, fill with the cream, and dust with powdered sugar.

Financier

Ingredients:

- 100 g butter
- 125 g almond flour
- 75 g flour
- 200 g powdered sugar
- 4 egg whites
- A pinch of salt
- 1 tsp vanilla extract

Instructions:
Preheat oven to 200°C (400°F) and grease financier molds.
Melt butter until it turns golden brown and smells nutty.
Whisk together the almond flour, flour, powdered sugar, and salt.
Whisk in the egg whites, then add the melted butter and vanilla.
Pour the batter into molds and bake for 10–12 minutes until golden brown.
Allow to cool before serving.

Clafoutis

Ingredients:

- 500 g cherries (pitted)
- 2 eggs
- 100 g sugar
- 120 g flour
- 300 ml milk
- 1 tsp vanilla extract
- A pinch of salt

Instructions:
Preheat oven to 180°C (350°F).
Arrange the cherries in a buttered baking dish.
In a bowl, whisk together the eggs, sugar, flour, milk, vanilla, and salt until smooth.
Pour the batter over the cherries.
Bake for 30–35 minutes until the top is golden and puffed.
Serve warm with powdered sugar.

Opera Cake

Ingredients:

- **Biscuit Joconde:** 100 g almond flour, 100 g powdered sugar, 3 large eggs, 3 egg whites, 30 g flour, 30 g butter, melted

- **Coffee Syrup:** 50 ml water, 50 g sugar, 1 tbsp coffee

- **Buttercream:** 200 g butter, 200 g powdered sugar, 1 tsp vanilla extract

- **Ganache:** 100 g dark chocolate, 100 ml heavy cream

Instructions:
For the biscuit joconde, whisk eggs and sugar until thick and pale, then fold in almond flour, flour, and melted butter.
Beat egg whites and fold them gently into the batter.
Spread onto a baking sheet and bake at 200°C (400°F) for 10 minutes.
For the syrup, dissolve sugar in water and add coffee.
For the buttercream, beat butter and powdered sugar until fluffy, then add vanilla.
For the ganache, heat cream and pour over chopped chocolate.
Assemble the cake by layering biscuit joconde, coffee syrup, buttercream, and ganache.
Repeat layers, finishing with ganache.
Chill before serving.

Gâteau Basque

Ingredients:

- **Dough:** 250 g flour, 100 g sugar, 1 tsp baking powder, 1 pinch of salt, 125 g butter, 1 egg, 50 ml milk

- **Filling:** 200 g pastry cream (made with 250 ml milk, 2 egg yolks, 50 g sugar, 1 tbsp flour)

Instructions:
Preheat oven to 180°C (350°F).
Mix the dough ingredients and refrigerate for 30 minutes.
Roll out the dough and line a tart pan.
Fill with pastry cream, then cover with another layer of dough.
Bake for 30–35 minutes until golden.
Allow to cool before serving.

Gâteau Saint-Honoré

Ingredients:

- **Pâte à Choux:** 250 ml water, 100 g butter, 150 g flour, 3 eggs, 1 pinch of salt

- **Pastry Cream:** 500 ml milk, 100 g sugar, 4 egg yolks, 40 g cornstarch, 1 tsp vanilla extract

- **Caramel:** 150 g sugar, 1 tbsp water

Instructions:
Preheat oven to 200°C (400°F).
For the pâte à choux, bring water, butter, and salt to a boil.
Add flour and stir until a dough forms.
Add eggs one at a time, then pipe into small balls and bake for 25 minutes.
For the pastry cream, whisk sugar, egg yolks, cornstarch, and milk in a saucepan. Cook until thick, then cool.
For caramel, melt sugar with water until golden, then dip the choux balls into the caramel.
Assemble the cake by placing the caramelized choux balls around the pastry cream-filled center.

Chiffon Cake

Ingredients:

- 250 g cake flour
- 200 g sugar
- 1 tbsp baking powder
- ½ tsp salt
- 6 large eggs, separated
- 180 ml vegetable oil
- 180 ml water
- 1 tsp vanilla extract
- 1 tsp cream of tartar

Instructions:
Preheat oven to 175°C (350°F).
In a large bowl, sift together the cake flour, sugar, baking powder, and salt.
In a separate bowl, whisk egg yolks, oil, water, and vanilla.
Gradually add the wet ingredients to the dry ingredients, mixing until smooth.
In another bowl, beat egg whites with cream of tartar until stiff peaks form.
Fold the egg whites into the batter.
Pour the batter into an ungreased tube pan and bake for 45–50 minutes.
Cool the cake upside down, then remove from the pan.
Serve as is or with a light glaze.

Tarte au Citron (Lemon Tart)

Ingredients:

- **Pastry:** 250 g flour, 125 g butter, 75 g sugar, 1 egg
- **Filling:** 4 large eggs, 150 g sugar, 1 tsp lemon zest, 180 ml fresh lemon juice, 200 ml heavy cream

Instructions:

Preheat oven to 180°C (350°F).
For the pastry, mix flour, butter, sugar, and egg into a dough.
Roll out the dough and press it into a tart pan.
Bake for 10–12 minutes until golden and crisp.
For the filling, whisk eggs, sugar, lemon zest, and juice in a bowl.
Add cream and whisk again.
Pour the filling into the baked crust and bake for 15–20 minutes until set.
Let cool and serve with whipped cream or berries.

Gâteau de Mamie (Grandmother's Cake)

Ingredients:

- 250 g flour
- 200 g sugar
- 1 tsp baking powder
- 1 tsp vanilla extract
- 100 g melted butter
- 2 large eggs
- 120 ml milk

Instructions:
Preheat oven to 180°C (350°F).
Mix flour, sugar, and baking powder in a bowl.
In a separate bowl, whisk eggs, melted butter, milk, and vanilla.
Combine both mixtures and pour into a greased cake pan.
Bake for 25–30 minutes, or until a toothpick comes out clean.
Serve with a dusting of powdered sugar or a simple glaze.

Gâteau au Yaourt (Yogurt Cake)

Ingredients:

- 1 pot of plain yogurt (around 150 g)
- 2 pots sugar
- 3 pots flour
- 1 pot vegetable oil
- 3 large eggs
- 1 tsp vanilla extract
- 1 tsp baking powder

Instructions:

Preheat oven to 180°C (350°F).
Use the yogurt pot as a measure for the other ingredients.
In a bowl, whisk the yogurt, eggs, and sugar together.
Add flour, baking powder, and oil, mixing until smooth.
Pour the batter into a greased cake pan and bake for 30–35 minutes.
Let cool and serve with a dusting of powdered sugar or fruit.

Baba au Rhum

Ingredients:

- 250 g flour
- 125 g butter
- 50 g sugar
- 3 eggs
- 20 g yeast
- 100 ml milk
- 100 ml rum
- 200 ml syrup (sugar and water)

Instructions:
Preheat oven to 180°C (350°F).
Dissolve yeast in warm milk and let it sit for 10 minutes.
In a bowl, mix flour, butter, sugar, and eggs, then add the yeast mixture.
Let the dough rise for about 30 minutes.
Spoon the dough into a greased baba mold and bake for 25–30 minutes.
While the baba is baking, prepare the syrup by dissolving sugar in water and adding rum.
Once the baba is baked, soak it in the rum syrup for a few minutes before serving.

Tartelette au Chocolat

Ingredients:

- **Pastry:** 250 g flour, 125 g butter, 75 g sugar, 1 egg

- **Filling:** 200 g dark chocolate, 200 ml heavy cream, 2 tbsp sugar

Instructions:
Preheat oven to 180°C (350°F).
For the pastry, mix flour, butter, sugar, and egg into a dough.
Roll out the dough and press it into tartlet pans.
Bake for 10–12 minutes until golden.
For the filling, heat the cream and pour it over chopped chocolate.
Stir until smooth, then pour the chocolate into the cooled pastry shells.
Chill before serving.

Kouign-Amann

Ingredients:

- 250 g flour
- 250 g butter
- 200 g sugar
- 100 ml water
- 1 tsp yeast
- A pinch of salt

Instructions:
In a bowl, mix flour, yeast, and salt.
Add water and knead until smooth.
Let the dough rise for 1 hour.
Roll out the dough and spread softened butter over it.
Sprinkle sugar on top, fold the dough, and roll it up.
Let it rise for another 30 minutes, then bake at 200°C (400°F) for 30–35 minutes until golden and caramelized.

Dacquoise

Ingredients:

- 200 g almond flour
- 200 g sugar
- 4 egg whites
- 1 tsp vanilla extract
- 100 g whipped cream

Instructions:

Preheat oven to 180°C (350°F).
Whisk egg whites until stiff peaks form.
Fold in sugar and almond flour.
Spread the mixture into two circles on a parchment-lined baking sheet.
Bake for 30–35 minutes, or until golden.
Once cool, sandwich the two layers with whipped cream and serve.

Mousse au Chocolat Cake

Ingredients:

- **Chocolate Cake:** 200 g dark chocolate, 100 g butter, 4 large eggs, 150 g sugar, 100 g flour

- **Mousse:** 200 g dark chocolate, 300 ml heavy cream, 2 tbsp sugar

Instructions:
Preheat oven to 175°C (350°F).
For the cake, melt the butter and chocolate.
Whisk eggs and sugar until fluffy, then fold in the chocolate mixture and flour.
Pour into a greased cake pan and bake for 25–30 minutes.
For the mousse, melt the chocolate and stir in the sugar.
Whip the cream and fold it into the chocolate.
Once the cake has cooled, top with the mousse and chill for at least 2 hours before serving.

Gâteau de Savoie

Ingredients:

- 6 large eggs
- 200 g sugar
- 200 g flour
- 1 tsp baking powder
- 1 tsp vanilla extract
- A pinch of salt

Instructions:
Preheat oven to 180°C (350°F).
Whisk the eggs and sugar until pale and fluffy.
Sift together the flour, baking powder, and salt.
Fold the dry ingredients into the egg mixture gently, then add the vanilla extract.
Pour the batter into a greased and floured cake pan.
Bake for 25–30 minutes until golden and a toothpick comes out clean.
Let cool before serving, dusted with powdered sugar if desired.

Gâteau au Miel (Honey Cake)

Ingredients:

- 250 g flour
- 100 g sugar
- 1 tsp baking powder
- 1 tsp cinnamon
- 3 large eggs
- 150 g honey
- 100 ml vegetable oil
- 1 tsp vanilla extract

Instructions:
Preheat oven to 180°C (350°F).
In a bowl, mix the flour, sugar, baking powder, and cinnamon.
In another bowl, whisk together the eggs, honey, oil, and vanilla extract.
Combine the wet and dry ingredients, mixing until smooth.
Pour the batter into a greased cake pan and bake for 30–35 minutes.
Let the cake cool before serving with a drizzle of honey on top.

Cannelé

Ingredients:

- 500 ml milk
- 2 eggs
- 200 g sugar
- 100 g flour
- 50 g butter
- 1 tsp vanilla extract
- 2 tbsp dark rum

Instructions:

Preheat oven to 220°C (430°F).
Heat the milk and butter in a saucepan until the butter melts, then let it cool.
Whisk together the eggs, sugar, flour, vanilla, and rum.
Add the cooled milk mixture and stir until smooth.
Grease and flour cannelé molds, then fill each mold with the batter.
Bake for 50–60 minutes until golden brown and crisp on the outside.
Allow the cannelés to cool before serving.

Galette des Rois

Ingredients:

- 2 sheets puff pastry
- 100 g almond flour
- 100 g sugar
- 100 g butter, softened
- 2 large eggs
- 1 tsp vanilla extract
- 1 egg (for egg wash)

Instructions:
Preheat oven to 200°C (400°F).
In a bowl, mix the almond flour, sugar, butter, eggs, and vanilla to make the almond cream.
Roll out one sheet of puff pastry and spread the almond cream on top, leaving a border around the edges.
Place the second sheet of puff pastry on top and press the edges to seal.
Brush the top with beaten egg for a golden finish.
Bake for 25–30 minutes until golden and puffed.
Let cool before serving.

Gâteau Bourdaloue

Ingredients:

- **Almond Cream:** 150 g almond flour, 100 g sugar, 100 g butter, 2 eggs, 1 tsp vanilla extract

- **Pastry:** 250 g flour, 125 g butter, 75 g sugar, 1 egg

- 4 pears, peeled and cored

Instructions:
Preheat oven to 180°C (350°F).
For the almond cream, beat together almond flour, sugar, butter, eggs, and vanilla extract until smooth.
For the pastry, mix flour, butter, sugar, and egg to form a dough.
Roll out the dough and line a tart pan.
Spread the almond cream into the tart shell.
Slice the pears and arrange them on top of the almond cream.
Bake for 40–45 minutes until the almond cream is set and golden.
Let cool before serving.

Tarte aux Poires (Pear Tart)

Ingredients:

- **Pastry:** 250 g flour, 125 g butter, 75 g sugar, 1 egg
- 4 pears, peeled and sliced
- 100 g sugar
- 200 ml heavy cream
- 1 tsp vanilla extract

Instructions:
Preheat oven to 180°C (350°F).
For the pastry, mix the flour, butter, sugar, and egg to form a dough.
Roll out the dough and line a tart pan.
Arrange the pear slices in a spiral pattern over the pastry.
Mix the sugar, cream, and vanilla extract and pour over the pears.
Bake for 30–35 minutes until the pastry is golden and the pears are tender.
Let cool before serving.

Cake de Pâques (Easter Cake)

Ingredients:

- 200 g flour
- 150 g sugar
- 3 large eggs
- 100 g butter, melted
- 1 tsp vanilla extract
- 100 ml milk
- 1 tsp baking powder
- 100 g candied fruits (optional)

Instructions:

Preheat oven to 180°C (350°F).
Whisk the eggs and sugar together until pale.
Add the melted butter, vanilla extract, and milk.
Fold in the flour and baking powder until smooth.
Add the candied fruits, if desired, and mix well.
Pour the batter into a greased cake pan and bake for 30–35 minutes.
Allow the cake to cool before serving, optionally dusted with powdered sugar.

Pithiviers

Ingredients:

- 2 sheets puff pastry
- 200 g almond paste
- 100 g sugar
- 1 egg
- 1 tsp vanilla extract

Instructions:
Preheat oven to 200°C (400°F).
Roll out one sheet of puff pastry and place on a baking sheet.
Mix almond paste, sugar, egg, and vanilla extract to make the filling.
Spread the filling over the pastry, leaving a border around the edges.
Place the second sheet of puff pastry on top and press the edges to seal.
Brush the top with beaten egg for a golden finish.
Bake for 25–30 minutes until golden and puffed.
Let cool before serving.

Tarte au Praliné

Ingredients:

- **Pastry:** 250 g flour, 125 g butter, 75 g sugar, 1 egg
- 200 g praline paste
- 100 ml heavy cream

Instructions:
Preheat oven to 180°C (350°F).
For the pastry, mix flour, butter, sugar, and egg into a dough.
Roll out the dough and line a tart pan.
Bake the pastry for 10–12 minutes until golden and crisp.
Mix the praline paste and cream until smooth.
Pour the praline mixture into the baked pastry shell.
Chill for 2 hours before serving.

Pain d'Épices

Ingredients:

- 250 g flour
- 200 g honey
- 100 g sugar
- 1 tsp baking powder
- 1 tsp cinnamon
- 1 tsp ginger
- 1 tsp nutmeg
- 2 eggs
- 100 ml milk
- 50 g butter

Instructions:
Preheat oven to 180°C (350°F).
In a bowl, whisk together the flour, baking powder, and spices.
In another bowl, combine honey, sugar, eggs, milk, and melted butter.
Gradually add the dry ingredients to the wet ingredients and mix until smooth.
Pour the batter into a greased loaf pan and bake for 45–50 minutes.
Let cool before slicing and serving.

Tarte aux Fruits Rouges (Red Berry Tart)

Ingredients:

- **Pastry:** 250 g flour, 125 g butter, 75 g sugar, 1 egg
- 200 g mixed red berries (strawberries, raspberries, blueberries)
- 150 ml heavy cream
- 100 g sugar
- 1 tsp vanilla extract

Instructions:
Preheat oven to 180°C (350°F).
For the pastry, mix flour, butter, sugar, and egg into a dough.
Roll out the dough and line a tart pan.
Bake for 10–12 minutes until golden.
For the filling, whisk together heavy cream, sugar, and vanilla extract until soft peaks form.
Spread the whipped cream over the baked pastry shell.
Top with the mixed red berries and refrigerate for an hour before serving.

Moelleux au Chocolat (Chocolate Lava Cake)

Ingredients:

- 200 g dark chocolate
- 150 g butter
- 3 large eggs
- 100 g sugar
- 50 g flour
- A pinch of salt

Instructions:

Preheat oven to 180°C (350°F).
Melt the chocolate and butter together over a double boiler.
In a bowl, whisk the eggs and sugar until fluffy.
Add the melted chocolate mixture and flour, stirring until smooth.
Pour the batter into greased ramekins and bake for 10–12 minutes until the edges are set but the center is still soft.
Serve immediately, topped with a scoop of vanilla ice cream or whipped cream.

Crêpe Cake

Ingredients:

- **For the crêpes:**
    - 250 g flour
    - 2 eggs
    - 500 ml milk
    - 50 g butter
    - 1 tbsp sugar
    - A pinch of salt
- **For the filling:**
    - 500 ml whipped cream
    - 100 g sugar
    - 1 tsp vanilla extract

Instructions:
Make the crêpes by whisking together flour, eggs, milk, melted butter, sugar, and salt until smooth.
Cook the crêpes in a non-stick skillet, flipping them once they set on the edges, and cook for about 2 minutes per side.
Stack the crêpes as you go, allowing each one to cool.
For the filling, whip the cream with sugar and vanilla until stiff peaks form.
Once the crêpes are stacked, spread a thin layer of whipped cream between each crêpe.
Chill the cake for 1 hour before serving.

Flan Parisien (Parisian Flan)

Ingredients:

- 1 sheet puff pastry
- 500 ml milk
- 150 g sugar
- 4 large eggs
- 50 g cornstarch
- 1 tsp vanilla extract

Instructions:
Preheat oven to 180°C (350°F).
Roll out the puff pastry and line a tart pan.
In a saucepan, heat the milk and sugar until the sugar dissolves.
In a bowl, whisk the eggs, cornstarch, and vanilla.
Slowly add the hot milk to the egg mixture, whisking constantly.
Pour the mixture into the pastry shell and bake for 40–45 minutes until set and golden on top.
Let cool before serving.

Soufflé au Chocolat (Chocolate Soufflé)

Ingredients:

- 200 g dark chocolate
- 4 large eggs
- 100 g sugar
- 100 ml milk
- 50 g butter
- 1 tsp vanilla extract

Instructions:
Preheat oven to 200°C (400°F).
Melt the chocolate and butter together.
In a separate bowl, whisk the egg yolks with sugar and vanilla.
Add the melted chocolate mixture to the egg yolks and mix well.
Whisk the egg whites to stiff peaks and fold them gently into the chocolate mixture.
Spoon the batter into greased soufflé dishes and bake for 10–12 minutes.
Serve immediately, dusted with powdered sugar.

Tarte aux Noix de Pécan (Pecan Pie)

Ingredients:

- **Pastry:** 250 g flour, 125 g butter, 75 g sugar, 1 egg
- 200 g pecans
- 200 g brown sugar
- 3 large eggs
- 100 ml corn syrup
- 50 g butter, melted
- 1 tsp vanilla extract

Instructions:
Preheat oven to 180°C (350°F).
For the pastry, mix flour, butter, sugar, and egg into a dough.
Roll out the dough and line a tart pan.
In a bowl, whisk the eggs, sugar, corn syrup, melted butter, and vanilla.
Stir in the pecans and pour the mixture into the pastry shell.
Bake for 35–40 minutes until the filling is set.
Let cool before serving.

Gâteau Opéra

Ingredients:

- **For the almond sponge:**
    - 150 g almond flour
    - 150 g sugar
    - 4 large eggs
    - 50 g flour
    - 1 tsp baking powder

- **For the coffee syrup:**
    - 100 ml water
    - 100 g sugar
    - 2 tbsp instant coffee

- **For the buttercream:**
    - 200 g butter
    - 200 g powdered sugar
    - 50 g dark chocolate
    - 2 tbsp coffee syrup

Instructions:
Preheat oven to 180°C (350°F).
For the almond sponge, whisk together the eggs and sugar.
Fold in the almond flour, flour, and baking powder.

Bake the sponge in a 20x20 cm pan for 10-12 minutes.
For the coffee syrup, boil water and sugar, then stir in the coffee.
For the buttercream, beat the butter and powdered sugar until fluffy, then add melted chocolate and coffee syrup.
Once the sponge is baked and cooled, cut into layers.
Layer the sponge, coffee syrup, and buttercream in a rectangular pan, finishing with a layer of buttercream.
Chill before serving.

Quatre-Quarts (Pound Cake)

Ingredients:

- 250 g butter, softened
- 250 g sugar
- 250 g flour
- 4 large eggs
- 1 tsp vanilla extract

Instructions:
Preheat oven to 180°C (350°F).
In a bowl, cream the butter and sugar together until fluffy.
Add the eggs one at a time, mixing well after each addition.
Fold in the flour and vanilla extract.
Pour the batter into a greased loaf pan and bake for 45–50 minutes until golden and a toothpick comes out clean.
Let cool before serving.

Charlotte aux Fraises (Strawberry Charlotte)

Ingredients:

- 1 package ladyfingers
- 500 g fresh strawberries, hulled and sliced
- 200 ml heavy cream
- 100 g sugar
- 1 tsp vanilla extract
- 2 tbsp strawberry jam
- 2 tbsp water
- 2 tbsp gelatin

Instructions:
Whip the cream with sugar and vanilla extract until stiff peaks form.
In a saucepan, heat the water and strawberry jam, then dissolve the gelatin in the warm mixture.
Allow it to cool slightly before folding it into the whipped cream.
Line a round cake mold with ladyfingers, ensuring they cover the sides.
Place a layer of strawberries at the bottom, then pour a layer of whipped cream mixture over.
Repeat the layers, finishing with whipped cream.
Chill in the fridge for at least 4 hours or overnight.
Decorate with whole strawberries before serving.

Mousse au Pistache Cake

Ingredients:

- **For the cake:**
    - 200 g flour
    - 150 g sugar
    - 4 large eggs
    - 50 g butter, melted
    - 1 tsp vanilla extract
    - 1 tsp baking powder
- **For the pistachio mousse:**
    - 200 g pistachio paste
    - 300 ml heavy cream
    - 100 g sugar
    - 3 gelatin sheets

Instructions:
Preheat oven to 180°C (350°F).
For the cake, beat the eggs and sugar until light and fluffy, then fold in the melted butter, vanilla, flour, and baking powder.
Pour into a greased cake pan and bake for 25–30 minutes until a toothpick comes out clean.
For the mousse, dissolve the gelatin sheets in cold water.
Whip the cream with sugar until stiff, then gently fold in the pistachio paste and dissolved gelatin.

Once the cake has cooled, spread a layer of pistachio mousse on top, then refrigerate for at least 4 hours before serving.

Tarte Normande

Ingredients:

- **For the pastry:**
    - 250 g flour
    - 125 g butter, cold
    - 75 g sugar
    - 1 egg
- 4 large apples, peeled and sliced
- 200 ml heavy cream
- 100 g sugar
- 1 tsp vanilla extract
- 2 eggs

Instructions:
Preheat oven to 180°C (350°F).
For the pastry, mix flour, butter, sugar, and egg to form a dough.
Roll out the dough and line a tart pan.
In a separate bowl, whisk the eggs, sugar, cream, and vanilla.
Place the apple slices in a spiral pattern over the tart shell.
Pour the cream mixture over the apples.
Bake for 40–45 minutes until golden and set.

Biscuit Joconde

Ingredients:

- 4 large eggs
- 100 g sugar
- 100 g almond flour
- 30 g all-purpose flour
- 3 egg whites
- 30 g sugar

Instructions:

Preheat oven to 200°C (400°F).
Whisk the eggs and sugar until fluffy, then fold in the almond flour and all-purpose flour.
In a separate bowl, beat the egg whites with sugar until stiff peaks form.
Gently fold the egg whites into the egg mixture.
Spread the batter onto a baking sheet lined with parchment paper and bake for 8–10 minutes.
Allow it to cool before using in layered cakes or desserts.

Tarte Bourdaloue

Ingredients:

- **For the pastry:**
    - 250 g flour
    - 125 g butter
    - 75 g sugar
    - 1 egg
- 4 pears, peeled and cored
- 100 g almond paste
- 100 g sugar
- 2 large eggs
- 1 tsp vanilla extract

Instructions:
Preheat oven to 180°C (350°F).
For the pastry, mix flour, butter, sugar, and egg to form a dough.
Roll out the dough and line a tart pan.
For the filling, whisk together almond paste, sugar, eggs, and vanilla.
Place the pear halves on top of the almond cream and pour the mixture over them.
Bake for 40–45 minutes until golden and set.

Pâte de Fruit Cake

Ingredients:

- 250 g fruit purée (such as raspberry or apricot)
- 150 g sugar
- 25 g pectin
- 50 g glucose syrup

Instructions:

In a saucepan, heat the fruit purée, glucose syrup, and sugar until it reaches a boil.
Stir in the pectin and cook for 5 minutes.
Pour the mixture into a mold and refrigerate until set.
Once firm, cut into cubes and use as a layer in cakes or as decorations.

Chouquette Cake

Ingredients:

- **For the pâte à choux:**
  - 125 g flour
  - 80 g butter
  - 250 ml water
  - 4 large eggs
  - A pinch of salt
  - Pearl sugar for topping
- 200 ml whipped cream
- 100 g chocolate ganache

Instructions:
Preheat oven to 180°C (350°F).
In a saucepan, heat the water, butter, and salt until the butter melts.
Add the flour and stir until the dough comes together.
Remove from heat, add the eggs one by one, stirring well after each.
Pipe small balls of dough onto a baking sheet and sprinkle with pearl sugar.
Bake for 25–30 minutes until puffed and golden.
Fill with whipped cream and drizzle with chocolate ganache.

Gâteau à la Crème de Marrons

Ingredients:

- 250 g chestnut purée
- 200 g sugar
- 4 large eggs
- 100 g butter, melted
- 150 g flour
- 1 tsp vanilla extract
- 1 tsp baking powder

Instructions:
Preheat oven to 180°C (350°F).
Whisk the eggs and sugar until fluffy.
Add the melted butter, chestnut purée, flour, vanilla, and baking powder.
Fold until smooth, then pour the batter into a greased cake pan.
Bake for 30–35 minutes until golden.
Let cool before serving.

Tarte aux Citron Vert (Key Lime Tart)

Ingredients:

- For the pastry:
    - 250 g flour
    - 125 g butter
    - 75 g sugar
    - 1 egg
- 5 large limes, juiced
- 400 ml sweetened condensed milk
- 4 large egg yolks

Instructions:
Preheat oven to 180°C (350°F).
For the pastry, mix flour, butter, sugar, and egg to form a dough.
Roll out the dough and line a tart pan.
In a bowl, whisk together lime juice, sweetened condensed milk, and egg yolks.
Pour the lime mixture into the prepared tart shell and bake for 15–20 minutes.
Chill for 2 hours before serving.

Flaugnarde

Ingredients:

- 3 large eggs
- 100 g (1/2 cup) sugar
- 1 pinch salt
- 90 g (3/4 cup) all-purpose flour
- 300 ml (1 1/4 cups) milk
- 1 tsp vanilla extract
- 2 tbsp melted butter
- 2–3 ripe pears or apples, sliced
- Powdered sugar, for dusting

Instructions:
Preheat oven to 180°C (350°F).
Whisk eggs with sugar and salt. Add flour gradually, then stir in milk, vanilla, and melted butter until smooth.
Grease a baking dish, spread the fruit evenly in it, then pour the batter over the fruit.
Bake for 35–40 minutes or until puffed and golden.
Cool slightly and dust with powdered sugar before serving.

Gâteau au Chocolat et à la Crème Fraîche

Ingredients:

- 200 g dark chocolate
- 150 g butter
- 100 g sugar
- 3 large eggs
- 100 g all-purpose flour
- 1 tsp baking powder
- 100 g crème fraîche

Instructions:

Preheat oven to 180°C (350°F).
Melt chocolate and butter together. Whisk eggs and sugar until light.
Stir in melted chocolate mixture, then sift in flour and baking powder.
Fold in crème fraîche until the batter is smooth.
Pour into a greased cake pan and bake for 25–30 minutes.
Let cool and dust with cocoa or serve with extra crème fraîche.

Savarin

Ingredients:

- 200 g flour
- 2 tbsp sugar
- 1 packet (7 g) dry yeast
- 2 large eggs
- 100 ml warm milk
- 80 g butter, softened
- Pinch of salt
- **For the syrup:**
  - 250 ml water
  - 150 g sugar
  - 2–3 tbsp dark rum

Instructions:
Mix flour, yeast, sugar, and salt. Add eggs and warm milk. Beat until smooth, then incorporate butter.
Let dough rise until doubled. Pour into a buttered ring mold and let rise again.
Bake at 180°C (350°F) for 25–30 minutes.
For syrup, heat water and sugar until dissolved, then add rum.
Soak warm cake in syrup, then cool and serve with whipped cream or fruit.

Tarte au Caramel Beurre Salé

Ingredients:

- 1 shortcrust pastry (pâte sucrée)
- 200 g sugar
- 80 g salted butter
- 150 ml heavy cream
- Pinch of sea salt

Instructions:

Blind-bake the tart shell at 180°C (350°F) for 15–20 minutes.
In a saucepan, melt sugar until amber-colored. Stir in butter, then gradually add cream (careful of splatter).
Stir in salt and let cool slightly before pouring into baked shell.
Refrigerate until set (at least 2 hours). Serve chilled.

Tarte à la Crème Pâtissière

Ingredients:

- 1 shortcrust pastry

- **For the crème pâtissière:**

    - 500 ml milk

    - 1 vanilla bean or 1 tsp extract

    - 4 egg yolks

    - 100 g sugar

    - 40 g cornstarch

    - 30 g butter

- Fresh fruit for topping (berries, kiwi, etc.)

Instructions:

Bake the tart shell and cool.
For pastry cream: Heat milk with vanilla. Whisk yolks, sugar, and cornstarch.
Pour hot milk over egg mixture slowly, then return to heat and stir until thick.
Stir in butter and let cool completely.
Fill the shell with pastry cream and top with fresh fruit. Optionally glaze with warmed apricot jam.

www.ingramcontent.com/pod-product-compliance
Lightning Source LLC
LaVergne TN
LVHW081322060526
838201LV00055B/2404